The Rainbow Factory

By: Isaiah Snyder

Dorrance Publishing Co
585 Alpha Drive
Pittsburgh, PA 15238
Visit our website at *www.dorrancebookstore.com*

ISBN: 979-8-8872-9272-4
eISBN: 979-8-8872- 9772-9

The Rainbow Factory
By: Isaiah Snyder

"Time to make a rainbow!" said Leo the Leprechaun happily as he headed toward the Rainbow Maker in the Rainbow Factory.

Leo flipped the switch to the Rainbow Maker and watched all the colors spring out, except one.

"Oh no!" thought Leo to himself as he looked at the missing color rainbow. "The light must have burnt out."

Leo made his way over to a little door and knocked on it. "Come in!" said a high-pitched voice.

"Hi Ellie!" said Leo as he opened the door. "One of the lights for the rainbow burnt out!"

Ellie the Elf scratched her head. "That's funny, I just replaced it yesterday." Ellie shrugged and walked over to a closet and pulled out a light bulb.

"Be careful!" said Ellie looking at Leo with a serious face. "This is the last light bulb I have and if anything happens to it, you will have to see Don!"

Leo nodded and as he was heading back to the Rainbow Maker he tripped and...

CLASH! The light bulb broke.

Leo cleaned up his mess and nervously walked to Don's office. Leo knocked and waited. "WHAT!?" boomed a voice from inside the office. "H-Hey Don!" said Leo with a shaky voice. "I need a light bulb."

The door swung open and a box slid out. "Thanks Do..." the door slammed shut.

DON

Leo took the light bulb out of the box and headed back to the Rainbow Maker.

Leo was almost there when he tripped again and... CLASH! "Oh no!" said Leo as he looked at the broken bulb.

Leo cleaned up his mess once again and slowly walked back to the Rainbow Maker.

Leo looked at the machine in disappointment, then something caught his eye. He looked at the light bulb and turned it to the right and it turned on.

"You're kidding!" said Leo.

www.ingramcontent.com/pod-product-compliance
Lightning Source LLC
Chambersburg PA
CBHW040120150726
48005CB00013B/1802